All Souls Ministry Series

2: The Church

Other titles in this series:

Cautionary Tales

Series Editor: David Porter

All Souls Ministry Series

2: The Church

Michael Baughen
Andrew Cornes
Richard Inwood
Roger Simpson

Series Editor: David Porter

Marshall Pickering

Marshall Morgan and Scott
Marshall Pickering
3 Beggarwood Lane, Basingstoke, Hants RG23 7LP,
UK

Copyright © 1987 Michael Boughen, Andrew Cornes,
Richard Inwood, Roger Simpson
First published in 1987 by Marshall Morgan and Scott
Publications Ltd
Part of the Marshall Pickering Holdings Group
A subsidiary of the Zondervan Corporation

British Library Cataloguing in Publication Data

Bible basics. – (All Soul's ministry series)
2: The Church
1. Bible – Commentaries
I. Porter, David, *1945* – II. Porter,
Tricia III. Series
220.6 BS491.2

ISBN 0–551–01380–X

Printed in Great Britain by
Hazell Watson & Viney Limited
Member of the BPCC Group, Aylesbury, Bucks.

Contents

Introduction to the Series

The All Souls Ministry Series is based on addresses originally given by the preaching team of All Souls Langham Place, in the heart of London's West End. All Souls is celebrated for the relevance and faithfulness of its contemporary biblical and teaching ministry; a reputation it has enjoyed ever since the pioneering work of its internationally-known Rector Emeritus, John R. W. Stott. The titles in this volume have been transcribed and edited from the All Souls Tape Library by David and Tricia Porter; the authors themselves have then prepared their material for print. A primary aim has been to preserve elements of the spontaneity of the original spoken word, while aiming at the wider audience of a reading public. Biblical quotations are from the Revised Standard Version. Quotations from the Greek text of Scripture follow the transliterations of Vine's *Expository Dictionary*.

Notes on the Contributors

MICHAEL BAUGHEN was Rector of all Souls, Langham Place before his appointment in 1982 as Bishop of Chester. A prominent figure within the church, his teaching and preaching ministry is enjoyed not only throughout his diocese but on a wider scale at the Keswick Convention where he is a regular and favourite speaker. He is author of many books, *Moses and the Venture of Faith, The Prayer Principle* (Mowbrays), and his Commentaries on 2 Timothy and 2 Corinthians, *Chained to the Gospel* and *Spiritual Health Warning* are published by Marshall Pickering. He is married to Myrtle; they have three children, Rachel, Phillip and Andrew, and one grandchild, Alexander. Michael is a railway, music, photography and travel enthusiast.

ANDREW CORNES is the Rector of the Church of the Ascension, Pittsburgh, Pennsylvania. He studied French and Russian at Corpus Christi College, Oxford and stayed on at Oxford, gaining a first in his Theology degree. He undertook further theological study at Durham University. He served a first curacy under David Watson at St Michael-le-Belfrey, York before becoming Director of

Training at All Souls and then Principal of the All Souls College of Applied Theology. He is married to Katherine, and they moved to the USA in 1985. His interests are travel and the theatre.

RICHARD INWOOD has been Vicar of St. Luke's, Bath since 1981. He was formerly on the staff of All Souls as Director of Pastoring, with a special interest in the development of Fellowship Groups. Before ordination he was a Research Chemist in industry. He writes regularly for Scripture Union's *Alive to God* Notes, and is the author of *Biblical Perspectives on Counselling* (Grove Pastoral Series, 1980) which was written while teaching a counselling course at All Souls. Richard is married to Liz, and they have three daughters, Hilary, Ruth and Alison. The Inwoods enjoy fellwalking and swimming as relaxations.

ROGER SIMPSON is one of the most outstanding of Britain's younger evangelists. He was Director of Evangelism at All Souls from 1979 to 1985. He travels widely, and has led missions throughout the UK, as well as in Australia, the United States and Switzerland. He is married to Mushy, and they have three children, Thomas, Mark and Mary Jane. Late in 1985 they moved to Edinburgh where Roger is now the leader of the rapidly growing St Paul's and St George's Church in the centre of the capital city. He is also a very able water-colour artist.

Preface

by Richard Bewes,
Rector of All Souls Church,
Langham Place.

'Are you suggesting, Vicar,' asked the curate, 'that I put more fire into my sermons?'

'No,' replied the vicar. 'I'm really trying to suggest that you put more of your sermons into the fire.'

That little dialogue is an apt commentary on the way that many of our contemporaries feel about preaching. The sermon seems to have nose-dived in popularity in recent years. If our preaching team at All Souls has agreed to present a little of our pulpit ministry in book form, I can only tell you that it took several months of negotiation and friendly persuasion before we hesitatingly agreed to the suggestion.

Any preacher will know why we are nervous! Few of us, looking back at the way in which we have expounded the sacred text of God's majestic revelation, feel proud of our efforts. Even the great missionary pioneer, Henry Martyn, had to concede after preaching one November in the village of Lolworth: 'But on reading over my sermon I was chilled and frozen by the deadness and stupidity of it.' (*My Love Must Wait*, IVP).

9

To those of us who preach it is always an amazement that the Spirit of God can touch and irradiate our poor efforts and make something of them. As you turn these pages, try to place yourself among the many who are present at any one of our main services at All Souls. Perhaps you are sitting there in the gallery – your particular situation, your struggles and your sins known to no one but God. There might even be an outsize crowd on a Sunday night, and you find yourself sharing the service by a closed-circuit television in the hall downstairs. In such a case, it is all being mediated to you, slightly second-hand – just as it is for those who live far away and hear the sermons through the services of our tape library.

The astounding thing is that God can still speak through the ancient biblical documents, cutting through the history and changing cultures of two thousand years, overcoming the obstacles presented by inadequate human communicators, by galleries and pillars, by microphones and television cameras, by the dehumanised technology of oxidised polyester tape – yes, and by the impersonal medium of a printed page. Can we believe that?

Why not? I began with a negative quote; let D. L. Moody supply us with a positive one: 'If you have got a sermon that is really good for anything, pass it round!'

Richard Bewes

1

What is the Church?

Michael Baughen

We are now beginning a series of studies in which we look at aspects of the corporate life of the people of God. We will be considering many of the concerns and indeed controversies that have arisen over many aspects of the Church.

First we need to ask the question: 'What is the Church?' Is it High, Low, Medium, Tepid, Catholic, Evangelical, Baptist, C of E, RC, Methodist, URC, House-Church, Brethren? Or is that not what is meant by 'the Church'?

When I was in one of the southern states of the USA, I went down one street where the number of different churches was mind-boggling. Each seemed to have a bigger notice board than the previous one, claiming to be 'The First, Apostolic, Evangelical, God-given this, that and the other' [and so on] 'Church of Jesus Christ'.

Very often, when people think of the Church, they think in those terms; a named, categorised, visible institution. But sometimes the word is used in other ways. If you look up towards the roof of All Souls you will see, high up in the building, some carved rosettes. When we rebuilt part of All Souls we took the opportunity to redecorate, and we tackled those rosettes. I remember standing on some scaffolding alongside the painter when he said to me, in a memorable moment, 'Of course – this isn't a proper church, is it?'

I held on to the scaffolding and took a deep breath! But it turned out that what he meant was that it wasn't pointed at the top. It wasn't Gothic. So it couldn't be a proper church.

He was typical of many people for whom the word 'church' simply means 'a building that happens to have a tower or a steeple'.

Then there's another use of the term, which is used when somebody is entering the ministry. On such occasions you will hear people say, 'Oh – Johnny's going into the Church'. (To which one is liable to reply, 'I thought he did that every Sunday!')

So there are a variety of ways in which the word 'church' is commonly understood. But the word 'Church' has a much greater significance than any of those interpretations, of course. The *Thirty-Nine Articles* of the Church of England, for example, explain that:

The visible Church of Christ is a congregation of faithful men in which the pure word of God is preached and the sacraments be duly ministered according to Christ's ordinance, in all those things that of necessity are requisite to the same (*Article XIX*).

A congregation of faithful men – and, of course, women – in which the pure word of God is preached and sacraments administered. That is the Church's own definition of the Church, and you can read it at the back of the Prayer Book, in the Articles.

The word that is used in the New Testament is the Greek word *ekklesia*, which means 'called out' or 'called together'. So immediately we see that it is not a matter of buildings, but of people. This is an important concept for us to understand.

I have been involved in a number of building projects in different churches, and that has meant discussing with several different congregations the rebuilding or alteration of their church buildings.

What I have often encountered in such situations is an entrenched opposition. 'You can't touch the church! It has been like this in all these years' – as if the church is the building to which people come, rather than the people – the Church – whom the building exists to serve. It seems tragic to me that many people believe that what matters is the church building. Buildings are the servants of the people. Here in All Souls we refurbished our building so that we could operate more effectively as a church family; for the Church of God (as we see in Ephesians chapter 1) is people.

A God-committed People

The people of the Church are the people of God: his vineyard, his bride, his kingdom, his body, his building, his flock, his household, his temple – all these descriptions flow through the New Testament. They are all *his*.

So the Church is a people who are God-committed. From Ephesians chapters 1 and 2 we can see that we are God-committed in two specific ways.

Submission to the leadership

We are committed to Jesus as the head of the Church. Where he uses the term 'the body' – for example in Ephesians 1:23 – Paul is not expounding the fact that a body is composed of inter-related, inter-dependent members, but rather the fact that a body relates to the head in a specific way. We are 'his body', and we relate to him as a body to the head.

Now, if the body is cut from the head, it is totally ineffective. It is entirely dependent on the head. The head of the Church, Jesus Christ, is the one who directs and arranges and pulls together the different elements and parts of his body.

One of the most effective illustrations is that of an orchestra. When we have our orchestra playing in church we can see a body of people, each with different gifts. And yet those gifts, diverse though they are, are submitted to the direction of the leader. This calls for effective *leadership*, but it also calls for effective *submission* by the orchestra to the leader. Without that submission, someone playing the trombone could decide to have a real blaze-up in the middle of a flute solo, just to show that *he* was the trombonist in the orchestra. But no, the orchestra submits to the leader.

So both leadership and submission are needed, and in the Church of Jesus Christ the same is true. The effective leadership is not in doubt; but the submission to that leadership is a matter that often has to be faced by the body in any of its local manifestations.

We are members of his body; members, in a sense, of one of his local orchestras. The way the music is played (if I may use the illustration) may be very different in style from another church down the road, because that is what the leader requires. Consequently, each church in each community is constantly forced back to its knees, to say to the head of the Church: 'Lord, what is your will and your direction in this place?'

And so if our church is to be continually effective, it must continually come in prayer to God to say 'Lord, what is your will?' The prayer gathering is absolutely vital to the life of any church. Without it we might as well close down everything else we do. It is the hub, the heart of the church's life, where we say to the Lord 'Come amongst us, lead us, direct us, adjust us and correct us.'

This is part, isn't it, of the exciting stimulus that you get in the Acts of the Apostles. 'It seemed good to the Holy Spirit and to us' – the way in which God closes doors and opens them, directs people, and sends the Church out, or uses situations to get missionaries out, to different parts of the world. It is the Lord directing the Church. And he is the same Lord today, directing his Church in Bhutan, in Manoram, in London, or wherever it happens to be.

As the Rector of a church, I find that exciting and immensely consoling. If I were ultimately responsible for my church, I would have had a nervous breakdown at least eight years ago. But mercifully I am not. The Lord is! And as I brood upon the problems facing us at the moment, I know that the Lord has a plan. We know that together – don't we? – as a family. *He* is responsible for *his* Church.

Submission to the foundation

'[You are] built upon the foundation of the apostles and prophets, Christ Jesus himself being the cornerstone' (Ephesians 2.20).

The effective church is not only committed to the leadership of the Lord, but to the sure, certain and immovable foundation that God, in his own wisdom, has laid for us to build upon.

The foundation, as Paul says, is of course Jesus Christ himself, and his truth – his gospel, established by the apostles and the prophets as they passed it from mouth to mouth and group to group before the New Testament was eventually finalised.

Some strange aberrations within the House Church movement claim that the succession to the New Testament apostles is to be found in the appointing of further 'apostles' today and that such 'apostles' are equivalent to those of the New Testament. But it's not true.

The successors to the apostles are the books of the New Testament. This is the apostolic truth, and the contents of the New Testament were either apostolically written, or carry apostolic testimony. So the 'apostolic succession' – that strange phrase – does not consist of the laying on of hands, like a conduit through history, but it consists instead of the handing on of the truth of Jesus Christ as enshrined in the New Testament.

It is the succession of apostolic truth. And the leaders of the Church are committed both to guard the truth and to build the Church upon that truth. That is our task. That is why we preach the word, we come back to the word, we study the word, we apply our lives by the word, and we seek to think it through together. There is no other foundation.

Again, going back to the Articles of the Church of England we read:

> The Church has power to decree rites or ceremonies and authority in controversies of faith; and yet it is not lawful for the Church to ordain anything that is contrary to God's word written, neither may it so expound one place of Scripture, that it be repugnant to another (*Article XX*).

The Church is to be a witness and a keeper of Holy Writ, not an alterer. That's what we stand on. So we submit to the leadership of the living head of the Church and we stand upon the foundation he's given us for all time. Nobody's going to write another Bible. God has given it to us for all time. This is our authority, this is the rock on which our feet must stand; and we submit to that, our living Lord and his word.

A God-created people

I find this exciting! Nobody sat down and said, 'Let's start a Church.' What we are is a people, across the world, and indeed across now and eternity, which has been created by God. That makes it absolutely unique. Nobody could make another. There's no other community like it in all history. You get the force of this in these verses.

'You are no longer strangers and sojourners, but you are fellow citizens with the saints and members of the household of God' (Ephesians 2.19).

Many people were fascinated with the television programme 'Roots', which showed a black American tracing his family back through the generations. Our roots as Christians go back to Abraham. He's our great-great-great (and lots more 'greats') grandfather. That's where the Church began, not on the day of Pentecost. And way back, we see our God promise to Abraham that he will provide a people: 'I will make a covenant with you, make you the father of a multitude of nations.'

This promise was given and sealed. God spoke of Israel as his family. 'You only have I known of all the families on earth,' he said through Amos. That sense of 'his people' is carried on nationally and in a personal way through the prophecies of Jeremiah and Ezekiel. Eventually it comes to fruition for us in the New Testament, in the cross of Jesus Christ.

And so suddenly the great Old Testament inheritance, the idea of 'the people of God', is altered. Now it means both Jew and Gentile, who both come to God through Jesus Christ and his cross. And the whole powerful driving force of that, according to the first two chapters of Ephesians, lies in the fact that it is God who has done this thing. He has blessed you (1:3), destined you (1:5), redeemed you (1:7), purposed you (1:9–10), sealed you with the Holy Spirit (1:13); this is the God who has made you alive (2:5), this is the God who has been rich in mercy towards you (2:7), you are his workmanship (2:10); this is the God who in Christ Jesus has broken down barriers of hostility (2:14).

It's all God's creation. Now the great promises to the people of God are inherited by everybody who believes, Jew or Gentile. This is expressed in a very particular way in 1 Peter:

'You are a chosen race, a royal priesthood, a holy nation . . .' (1 Peter 2:9). These promises now are ours as Christians. We have access to the Father by Christ in the one Spirit. Are you excited about that?

I believe that we do need to have this deep sense that we are in a purpose of God that goes right the way back. When we become Christians we need to wake up to this. We are part of a vast family. As many as the stars of the sky or the sand of the seashore: that's what the kingdom of God is like. It is a family with whom we're going to spend eternity, and we'll have lots of 'time' to enjoy it.

So it's important when we become Christians, and thereby find ourselves part of the eternal Church of Jesus Christ, that we learn about our family. We need to go round the family portrait gallery. Here you are, here's great great Grandad Abraham; this is Grandad Moses, look what he did; here's Uncle Elijah, and Auntie Ruth, and Uncle Peter and Auntie Mary and Elizabeth; and Uncle Augustine and Uncle Luther; Auntie Corrie Ten-Boom – you can go on endlessly. They are all our relatives! Thousands and thousands of men and women of all different colours are part of the family that God promised to Abraham, in the covenant of promise. Isn't it glorious? We are a people created by him. We didn't decide it, we didn't make it, God didn't say 'You choose me.' He chose us.

The implications of being in the family, this 'household of God', are of course those of unity and love and brotherhood and sisterhood. Those are the things we'll be looking at in this series – serving,

19

using our gifts, being responsible, having care and concern and so on. And I hope we can really rejoice at being part of this togetherness called the 'family of God'.

When C. S. Lewis was a young man he had great difficulty in grasping this aspect of the Church. He confessed:

> I liked clergymen as I liked bears, and I have as little wish to be in the Church as in a zoo. There was to begin with a kind of collective, a wearisome get-together affair. I couldn't see that a concern of that sort should have anything to do with one's spiritual life. To me, religion ought to have been a matter of good men praying alone and meeting by twos and threes to talk of spiritual matters. None of the fussy time-wasting botheration of it all; the bells, the crowds, the umbrellas, the notices, the bustle, the perpetual arranging and organising. Hymns were, and are, extremely disagreeable to me, and of all musical instruments I liked, and like, the organ least.

He learnt a bit more about it later on! And I hope that being part of the Church family will be a wonderful experience for you, as it is for me.

A God-purposed people

'The whole structure is joined together and grows into a holy temple in the Lord' (Ephesians 2:21).

The Church is not simply something in which to sit and to enjoy, though we have a right to enjoy it. We are also called to serve. That passage in 1 Peter which we looked at earlier goes on to say:

'You are a chosen race . . . that you may declare the wonderful deeds of him who called you out of darkness into his marvellous light' (1 Peter 2:9). You have a job to do, just as the people of God had in the beginning.

Being a structure
We will look at two expressions in Ephesians 2:21 and 22. One is 'the whole *structure* growing into a holy temple . . .' (2:21). Now 'structure' sounds static, doesn't it? I can point to an actual building and say, for example, 'There is the church of All Souls.' But the word used by Paul means something that moves. It's actually a building site, rather than the finished job. It's a *work of building* that's going on. Do you ever look through a crack in a hoarding and see the bulldozers moving, the cranes operating and all sorts of things happening? It's an active building site, and much is taking place.

This is the picture that is being used here. The whole structure is continuing to be built. It isn't finished, it won't be finished until God ceases this creation, and gathers his family with him in heaven. Meanwhile you and I are on a building site. We are part of the structure.

So we have a job to do. It's no use sitting down and saying 'Well, I did my bit ten years ago.' You must be involved now. It bewilders me that some Christians can sit around in the church for year after year and not do a thing. Really they need to be picked up, and spanked, to make them see that being in a church means being involved. Sometimes it means serving in a very mundane way, but that's part of what being in a family involves – doing the washing-up sometimes.

God calls us to be involved in spreading the Church, building the Church, and seeing the Church of God in this world growing, adapting, moving forward, evangelising, being salt in society, light in the darkness; converting, challenging, preaching and testifying, and in itself deepening and learning and growing. How many people say, 'I wish it were like it was ten years ago!' Really, it can't be. The Church is a dynamic force under the power of the Holy Spirit. It's got to move forward. And you and I are part of that growing structure.

Being a temple
The Church is also to become 'a holy *temple* of God in the Lord, in whom you also are built into it for a dwelling place of God in the Spirit' (2:22). That's a tremendous concept, because the picture here is not the great precincts of the temple, but the holy of holies, the inner shrine, into which the Shekinah glory came. 'And that,' says God 'is where I now dwell, not in the building but in my people.' And if the world in London, in the West End, in Bhutan – or wherever God happens to call us – is to see the glory of the Lord, it is only going to see it in his people. There is no other way by which the glory of the Lord can be shown. I long that our worship together as a church may go on deepening in its reality.

I was thrilled when I once received a letter from a group from Denmark who had visited London and worshipped with us at All Souls. They had a terrible crossing on the boat, they were feeling exhausted, and none of the group apart from the leader were Christians. But the leader was determined to bring them here. She said in her letter that it was the most marvellous part of their visit. They didn't follow the language very well, but enjoyed being welcomed, the singing – and the fact that people laughed here! That was a revelation to them.

Well, thank God that something of the glory of the Lord – and I choose the words deliberately – was manifested to them. May it go on being more so, we've got so far to go.

But more than that I long that that glory should be shown by the Church in its individual sense; that each of us, as part of the Body, should live it out in our place of work, in our homes and families.

God give us grace to show forth his glory!

So what is the Church? It is a people, a people that is God-committed, God-created and God-purposed. Or, if you like, a body submitted to the head, God's family enjoying its relationships, a building growing in usefulness. Are you part of his people? If you believe in the Lord Jesus Christ you are in the Church whether you like it or not. You are part of his body.

If you are part of his body, are you committed to it? In All Souls I often say to new-comers, 'Membership of this church happens when you stop talking about what "they" do at All Souls and start talking about what "we" do at All Souls.' So it is with the Church of Jesus Christ. When it is what 'we' are involved in rather than what 'they' are involved in, you are in, and you have taken on the responsibility.

Leslie Newbigin once described real membership of the Church as a position in which the Church is the total involvement of one's life, rather than merely being among the circles in which you move. A real member of God's Church does not list it along with the rugby club, the office and the home. For him or her, it means being part of the family of God.

If you are a member of the Church in that sense, then it means that wherever you go, in your work, your home, your journeys – you go as a member of the people of God. It is not a compartment of life. It is your total heritage as part of God's Church.

So let us be fully involved and committed, exercised in prayer as well as action, so that we who are part of God's people may be seen to be his people, to his glory.

2

Excellent *

'On this rock I will build my church'

Andrew Cornes

> I tell you, you are Peter, and on this rock I will build my church, and the powers of death shall not prevail against it. I will give you the keys of the kingdom of heaven, and whatever you bind on earth shall be bound in heaven, and whatever you loose on earth shall be loosed in heaven (Matt. 16:18–19).

Each of the three parts of Christendom has its patron saint. For the Protestants it's Paul, with his profound teaching, his clear conversion experience, and his constant insistence on justification by faith rather than works. For the Orthodox Church, it's John; the beloved disciple, the great mystic, with his vivid symbolism and his awesome book about heaven. And for the Roman Catholic, it's Peter, the apostle who seems to have lived his last years at Rome and was martyred there. Perhaps we Protestants have neglected Peter. We magnify Paul, and indeed we pay considerable attention to John, especially to his Gospel; but Peter has simply been squeezed out. A series such as this on 'the Church' forces us to redress the balance.

We have before us what Jesus said about the Church. It's quite clear that he was fully aware that he was founding a new people of God. He chose, for example, twelve disciples, and that appears to be in deliberate imitation of the twelve founding-fathers of the tribes of Israel. But it so happens he only uses the word 'church' on two occasions, of which this is one. And in this passage in Matthew, what Jesus says about the Church is closely linked to, and in fact is overshadowed by, what he says about Peter. So we can't avoid looking at this great man, and that Jesus foretold that Peter was going to be three things.

The first leader of the Church

Verse 18 tells us, in a well known sentence: 'I tell you, you are Peter, and on this rock I will build my church.' The Church was yet to be built up. Indeed, it was not really established yet. But the building would begin after the death and the resurrection of Christ and the sending of his Spirit. And Peter was to be the rock with which the building began, and on which it is founded.

That is the natural way to take this verse. Peter was the name given to Simon the fisherman by Jesus himself.[1] The name means 'a rock', and now Jesus explains why the name is so appropriate. It is on Simon Peter – Simon the rock – that Jesus will build his Church.

A number of people (not only Protestants, but the Reformers are prominent among them) have

1. Mark 3:16; John 1:42

26

not liked this teaching, and have tried to find ways round it.

They have argued that the rock on which Christ built his Church is Peter's faith, or that it is the truth expressed in verse 16; that Jesus is 'the Christ, the Son of the living God'.

Some have pointed to the fact mentioned in the RSV footnote, that the Greek word for Peter is '*Petros*', but that for the rock the word used is *petra*. Therefore, they argue, Peter can't be the rock, otherwise Jesus would have used exactly the same word in both instances. But this overlooks the fact that Jesus almost certainly *did* use the word in both instances. He spoke in Aramaic. The word for a rock is *kepha*, a feminine noun. This was normally translated in Greek as *petra*, another feminine noun. But when such a word was made into a man's name, it was natural in Greek to change the feminine ending into a masculine one. So Simon the fisherman would be called '*Petros*'. But what Jesus himself almost certainly said was: 'You are *kepha*, and on this *kepha* I will build my Church' – using the same word in both cases, and making it very difficult for us, in all honesty, to draw any conclusion except that Peter is the rock.

So what is Jesus saying? He is taking an image which is familiar to us from the rest of the New Testament – the picture of the Church, the people of God, as a building. This image is used in various ways in the New Testament. Very frequently Jesus is described as the cornerstone holding the whole building together.

But here the picture is used in a different way. Here, the rock on which the structure rests is Peter. Christ's Church will be built on him. And that,

27

indeed, is what happened. Peter may well have been the first man to whom the risen Jesus appeared (Luke 24:34 and 1 Corinthians 15:5 seem to suggest that). He was certainly commissioned by the risen Lord in John 21 to 'feed my sheep'. And in those vital early years of the Christian Church it was Peter who was the leader, the spokesman, the organiser, the disciplinarian, and, with John, the acknowledged figure-head. It was Peter who steered the Church through its troubled dangerous early days, and assured its continuity and its progress when Jesus was no longer present in the flesh. It was he – to return to the image – who was the foundation rock on which Christ build his Church.

But what made him fitted for this role? Was it his rock-like character, his steadiness amidst the buffetings, that made Jesus choose him as the rock? That is not what the context of the passage in Matthew suggests, and we mustn't do what is so often done, which is to wrench these verses from their context.

Jesus has asked in verse 15, 'Who do you say that I am?' It is a deliberate test. Peter replies (verse 16) 'You are the Christ, the Son of the living God.' Jesus then bursts into praise (verse 17): 'Blessed are you, Simon Bar-Jona! For flesh and blood has not revealed this to you, but my Father who is in heaven.' And it is in this context that he says that Peter is the rock on which he will build his Church.

So what makes Peter fitted to be the foundation rock, the first leader, is not his character, but his firm grasp of Jesus as the Messiah, the Son of the living God.

Now we must ask in what sense is the Church built on Peter today. The Roman Catholic answer is clear. Jesus gave Peter the primacy, the ultimate authority within his Church. This primacy was first exercised by Peter at Jerusalem, and he took this authority with him to Rome and handed it on to his Roman successors. It is therefore on the popes as successors of Peter, so the Roman Catholic Church teaches, that Christ continues to build his Church today.

This is not a side issue. It is on this understanding that the Roman Catholic Church bases its claim to be the sole true Church and the sole definer of doctrine. On the truth or falsity of this claim, the whole Roman Catholic structure of teaching stands or falls. I would be doing them an injustice if I said that these verses were their only argument. Nevertheless a great deal of weight is placed on Jesus' promise to Peter here.

But it seems to me that there are three flaws in the Roman Catholic understanding of these verses. Firstly, there is no evidence – either here or anywhere else in the New Testament – that the mother church, the centre of the universal Church, was transferred from Jerusalem to Rome in apostolic times. On the contrary, in so far as there *was* a mother church, the entire New Testament makes clear that it was at Jerusalem and nowhere else.

Secondly, it is quite clear that within Peter's lifetime, he himself relinquished his position of leadership at Jerusalem and it passed instead to James. Indeed, to judge from Galatians 2 verses 11–13, Peter regarded himself as under James's jurisdiction or leadership.

Thirdly, there is no mention anywhere in the

New Testament of Peter's successors inheriting Peter's powers, or of him having any authority to pass his apostleship on to others. On the contrary, only Christ could bestow apostleship, and must do so in a direct living encounter.[2] There is no promise that Christ will build his Church on anyone other than Simon Peter the fisherman.

To return to our question: In what sense is the Church built on Peter today? In one sense, it isn't. This verse is not referring to the Church today, but to the initial building of the Church and the foundation rock on which it would be begun. But if Peter was fitted to be the rock because he had come to see that Jesus was 'the Christ, the Son of the living God', then we are building – or being built – on that same foundation rock when we follow his teaching and his faith.

When theologians start saying that Jesus was not in any unique sense the Messiah – the Son of God – they automatically forfeit their place in Christ's Church. They've taken themselves far away from the great confession of Peter, after which Jesus calls him the rock on which his Church was to be built.

There may be some reading this who have never fully agreed to the truth that Jesus is the Christ, the Son of the living God. You may be worshipping week by week, you are welcome in a Christian building. But make no mistake, you are not yet part of Christ's Church; not until you join with

2. This is inspired by 1 Corinthians 9:1, 15:8–9. It is true that the place left vacant by Judas' treachery was filled (Acts 1:5–26) but there were clearly defined conditions, including that the replacement should be a 'witness of Christ's resurrection'. And the person who chose the replacement was neither Peter nor the whole body of Christians, but God.

Peter, the rock, in his faith. He is the rock on which Christ has built his Church. He is the first leader of the Church.

The first preacher of the Church

In verse 19 Jesus is again speaking directly to Peter when he says 'I will give you the keys of the kingdom of heaven.'

There is the closest connection between the kingdom of heaven (verse 19) and the Church (verse 18). The kingdom of heaven means 'the rule of God'. This rule by which God is acknowledged as undisputed king, this answer to our prayer 'Thy Kingdom come', will only be fully established at the end of time. But in the meantime there is a group of those who have placed themselves voluntarily under God's rule; the people of God, the Church.

The Church is now the sphere of God's kingdom, his rule. And Jesus gives Peter its keys.

What are the keys for? Not *primarily* for locking doors. It was Jesus' complaint against the Pharisees that they did precisely that.

'Woe to you, scribes and Pharisees, hypocrites! because you shut the kingdom of heaven against men; for you neither enter yourselves, nor allow those who would enter to go in' (Matt. 23:13).

No, these keys given to Peter were *primarily* for opening up.[3] His job, was to open the kingdom of heaven to all believers, to be the usher, beckoning

3. Interpretation of the picture of the 'keys' has been obscured by thinking that the 'keys' are used to 'bind' or 'loose'. In fact, the 'binding' and 'loosing' of the second part of verse 19 is a quite different image, making a different point.

in all who would respond, or to use simple terms, to be a preacher or an evangelist.

Many people think that Peter holds the keys to the heaven where God lives. That is why there are so many stories and jokes about arriving at the 'pearly gates' and meeting Peter there, who then decides whether you can be let in or not. That is also why Peter is always depicted in art with his keys. But this too is based on misunderstanding, for two reasons.

Firstly, this responsibility was not given to Peter for ever, but only for his life on earth. Verse 19 continues, 'and whatever you bind on earth shall be bound in heaven (that is, by God), and whatever you loose on earth shall be loosed in heaven'. This whole verse is talking about Peter's earthly ministry. It says nothing about his life thereafter.

Secondly, the kingdom of heaven is not heaven. Heaven, as it is used twice in verse 19, means the place where God lives. The kingdom of heaven, or the kingdom of God, is wherever God rules; and for the time being, its earthly manifestation is the people of God, the Church.

So Peter was given the job of opening up the kingdom of heaven and encouraging everyone to come in. He was to be one of the first preachers of the Church, and so he proved to be. On the day of Pentecost it was Peter who preached. In the first chapters of Acts, it was Peter who preached again and again and thousands believed. When it was time for the first Gentile to believe, as Peter himself recorded later, 'God made choice among you, that by my mouth the Gentiles should hear the word of the gospel and believe' (Acts 15:7). It may have been Paul who was apostle to the Gentiles and brought in the floods of converts, but it was Peter who opened the flood-gates with his keys.

Later he became a great missionary. He left Jerusalem and went to Antioch, and then very likely to Asia Minor, Corinth and Rome, and probably to many other places. He was indeed the first great preacher who opened up the kingdom of heaven.

Is there any sense in which we too can use these keys? In the major sense, again, no. This promise was made to Peter the fisherman, with nothing said about anyone else.

But there is a sense in which we are all to stand at the entrance to God's kingdom and welcome people. So let me ask you: what have you done to the doors of the kingdom of heaven? Have you shut them? Perhaps our unspoken attitude is that everyone, if they have a hope of making a Christian commitment, must become exactly like us. And so because they drink and swear and lie a bit, you've written off those we work with. They could never become Christians, we think; and our rather supercilious attitude tells them so. We've shut the door.

Or have you simply left the door unattended? It may be there are people we know who are standing at the door, who in their heart of hearts want to come in, but don't understand how; and we know nothing of this. We've never asked them what they feel about the Christian faith, never invited them to come with us to a service. We've never gone to the threshold to see if they are there. We've left the door unattended.

Or have you flung the door open? Have you stood at the door of the kingdom of heaven, stood where the Church, the people of God, meets the world and invited and beckoned and welcomed people in? Have you done all you can to tell your friends, to share with them, that the way to God is open, that all they have to do is come, and no one will be turned away?

Peter initially turned the keys in the lock and by his preaching opened up the kingdom of heaven.[4] It is our job to keep those doors wide open. He is the first preacher of the Church.

Keys sometimes have to be used to lock. Sometimes people do have to be excluded, at least temporarily, from the kingdom of heaven, from the church. And Jesus goes on to make that point. But to do so he leaves behind the image of 'the keys' and uses a quite different verbal picture: 'binding' and 'loosing'; and in the last half of verse 19, Jesus promises that Peter will be:

The first disciplinarian of the Church
He says to Peter: 'Whatever you bind on earth shall be bound in heaven, and whatever you loose on earth shall be loosed in heaven' (verse 19).

The words here, 'binding' and 'loosing', are the normal ones for tethering and untethering an animal, or tying up and untying a captive human. But they are also used, both in ancient writings of Jewish rabbis and in Matthew's gospel, for pronouncing that a person's sins still cling to him ('binding') or have been forgiven and removed from him ('loosing') and that the person is being excluded from, or readmitted to, the fellowship of believers.

4. This is not, of course, to deny the much more important truth that Jesus, by his death and resurrection, made entry into God's kingdom possible.

34

Christ foresaw that there would be in his Church false teachers as well as true guides in Christ, gross sinners as well as exceptionally holy men and women of God. He foresaw that discipline would be necessary in the Church, and he gave Peter responsibility as the first disciplinarian in the Church.

And this is exactly what we find in Acts. As early as Acts chapter 5, a couple named Ananias and Sapphira sold a piece of property and blatantly lied about how much it had been sold for. It was Peter who confronted them about their deceit; and when they persisted in lying, it was Peter who pronounced their judgement, and in fact both of them died.

Once more we face the question: is there any sense in which we too are to be disciplinarians, like Peter? Perhaps surprisingly, the answer in this case is: yes. The very words Jesus uses in verse 19 about Peter are spoken in Matthew 18:18 to all Christians, or rather to churches. Jesus says that, when a church member has sinned and refuses to acknowledge his sin, the church is to meet together and, through its leaders, to exclude the sinning member from the church fellowship.

We will look at this question, and at Matthew 18:15–20, in greater detail in chapter 5. However, we need to recognise at this stage that although Peter was the first and primary disciplinarian within the early Church, the responsibility for disciplining its erring members is placed on every church. And this is precisely what churches today are very loath to do.

A church member goes through a very painful and messy divorce in which her partner was far more to blame than she. Soon it transpires that she is not only seeing another man but sleeping with him from time to time. She is prepared to admit what she is doing but feels she desperately needs his comfort and support and will not give up having intercourse. It is great that normally, in the modern Church, our immediate reaction is to show understanding and compassion; but when that is accompanied by turning a blind eye to her sexual practice and taking no steps to confront her over her sin and discipline her, we are simply shirking the responsibility Christ has given us.

Again, a man has newly arrived in a church and, because of his obvious gifts and the training he claims to have received, is quickly given considerable leadership responsibility. It then comes out that he has told a whole string of lies, though he offers only lame explanations for what he has said and shows no signs of repentance. What most churches would do in these circumstances is try to hush the whole affair up; to bundle the man out of leadership and perhaps even out of the church, without telling the church members at a meeting of the Church, or exercising any public discipline. But this is a responsibility we cannot evade. Peter was commissioned as the first disciplinarian of the church, but all churches are also commissioned by Christ to discipline their sinning members.

So let us return to Peter: a great and, by Protestants, neglected man; the founding apostle about whom we should know more. His supreme privilege was this; he had bestowed upon him names which were elsewhere reserved only for God. Names like 'the rock', a term frequently used for God in the Old Testament, and in the New Testament for

Christ (e.g. 1 Cor. 10:4, 1 Pet. 2:8). Names like 'the keeper of the keys', for it's Jesus himself who declares in the book of the Revelation that 'I have the keys of Death and Hades' (Rev. 1:18). Again, Jesus calls himself 'The true one, who has the key of David, who opens and no one shall shut, who shuts and no one opens' (Rev. 3:7). Peter is chosen as God's founding representative, Christ's first great agent exercising some of God's own functions. Unique promises are made to him.

We cannot transfer to ourselves, or to others, all the promises made here to Peter. But we can follow in his footsteps. And we do, when we too hear Christ's question 'But who do you say that I am?' and gladly reply 'You are the Christ, the Son of the living God.'

3

The gates of hell will not prevail against it

Richard Inwood

In this study we will be looking at that phrase at the end of Matthew 16:18, which says, 'the powers of death shall not prevail against it', that is the Church. This is how the RSV translates it. A footnote indicates that 'the gates of Hades' is the strict translation from the Greek; the gates of Hades shall not prevail against the Church.

I think that the RSV translation in the main text, 'the powers of death', comes pretty close to what the verse is all about. It means that death has no power over the Church. Because of her Lord, and because of his conquest over death, she has burst the bonds of death; she has burst out of the gates of death which enslave the whole of mankind.

The powers of death

What then does this phrase 'the gates of Hades' or 'the powers of death' actually mean?

To grasp its meaning, we need to remind ourselves that the Old Testament view of what happened at death was very different from the view that we have today. In the Old Testament there is no clear-cut expectation of a concrete life after death. There appears to be a belief in a shadowy existence in the place of the dead, called 'Sheol' in the Old Testament, and 'Hades' in the Greek New Testament.

For example, in the book of Psalms the psalmist says that he prays that God won't let him go down into Sheol, into the pit. Or again, King Hezekiah was reprieved by God from death for fifteen years. He rejoices that this is so, and as he recalls what has happened to him, he says:

'I said, In the noontide of my days I must depart; I am consigned to the gates of Sheol for the rest of my years. I said, I shall not see the Lord in the land of the living' (Isa. 38:10–11).

Later in the same chapter, he says 'For Sheol cannot thank thee, death cannot praise thee; those who go down to the pit cannot hope for thy faithfulness' (Isa. 38:18).

So death is not seen as the end in the Old Testament, but it is, you might say, the 'worst best' thing. It's the thing which people fear most, because it's the end of a real, tangible life; you can't see anything beyond, you can't praise God from there. It's a miserable, shadowy existence. What really mattered to the men of the Old Testament was that they served their Lord here and now in this life. Death was an enemy to be avoided at all costs.

In the Old Testament, however, death is seen as a direct consequence of the sin of mankind, as it is in the New Testament. By sin, man was denied access to the tree of life. He was, in the language of Genesis 3, put out of the garden of Eden because of the fall. Indeed, as the New Testament has it, death is the wages of sin. Man is a slave to death because he is a slave to sin. Man can't be freed from death, because he has not yet been freed from sin. Death, then, is a pretty depressing business, if one does not take into account the subject matter of this study.

Tennessee Williams, the playwright, once observed that 'Man does not have the pig's advantage'. The pig's advantage is that it is completely unaware of its own mortality. It doesn't know that one day it's going to die. But we do, and man lives under the weight of the knowledge of his own death. One day the gates of the place of the dead will clang behind him, and there is nothing he can do about it. Man – because he *is* man – knows that he is mortal; and man, because he is man, can do nothing about it at all.

That's the depressing picture for man without Christ. I have painted it so, because I want to contrast it with the amazing thrust of this verse in Matthew 16.

Imagine the effect of these words upon the men of Jesus' day; particularly, of course, on Peter himself to whom they were spoken. Imagine what the effect would have been on men who had very little clear idea of something great and wonderful beyond death. They were told that they were part of a new community, the Church of Jesus founded on the foundation stones of the apostles and prophets, with Christ as the cornerstone; part of that community against which the powers of death were going to have no effect. No one else had ever burst through the powers of death. No one else had ever burst out of the gates of Sheol. But a time was coming, said Jesus, when there would be a

41

community who could and would do that. They would break out in the victory of their Saviour.

I think the imagery in this verse is really quite difficult. It is not easy to work out whether it's the Church that's doing the attacking against the gates of Hades, or whether it's the gates that are doing the attacking against the Church. Is it that the Church cannot be held in by the powers of death, but must attack and burst out of death? The gates can't prevail, that is, against the onslaught of the Church. Or is it that the foundation of the Church is so firm that whatever death throws at it, it's immovable? I don't think we can be sure which way round it is. In one sense both are true. Whichever it is, the meaning is the same. Death no longer wields any power over men and women who belong to the new community in the Lord Jesus Christ. Death is no longer an enemy; death no longer has the last word in a man's life; death is no longer a prison in which there is no escape.

The victory of life

So let us now turn from death to look at life, the opposite of death. That's what this verse invites us to do. It invites us to look at the past, at present and future aspects of this victory that there is over death and over the powers of death, in Christ.

Victory in the past

When Jesus first spoke these words, it was a case of 'the gates of Hades *shall* not prevail against it'; it was something in the future. The resurrection which broke the bonds of death had not yet taken place. But for us it has. For us, the proof of the power of Christ over the powers of death is abundantly plain. Jesus rose from the dead, or to be strictly accurate, God raised Jesus from the dead.

Acts chapter 2 is a particularly important passage; for two reasons. Firstly, it relates the resurrection of Jesus to the powers of death. And secondly, the speaker of this first Christian sermon on the day of Pentecost is Peter. I wonder whether, as Peter preached this sermon, he recalled the words that Jesus spoke to him which were recorded in Matthew 16? I wonder whether he remembered, as he preached about the powers of death being broken by the resurrection of Jesus, that Jesus had said to him 'On this rock I will build my church, and the gates of Hades will not prevail against it'? I think he would have had to be remarkably obtuse not to have seen the connection.

But what does this passage teach *us?*

I think it teaches us two things: firstly that the resurrection of Jesus is the key event in the conquest of the powers of death. And secondly that a person needs to be *in Christ*, needs to be *in the Church*, to share in it. Jesus is the forerunner of the Church. In this, as in everything else, he blazes the trail and we sweep in in the triumphal procession. When we become Christians we become incorporated into Christ. We become part of his Church, and we all share then in what happened to Christ on our behalf, as if we'd been there. We are united in his death and enjoy the benefits of that death, we are united in his resurrection and we are raised to new life in him, the new life that death can no longer touch. Jesus, says Peter in this sermon, fulfils the prophecy of David, that God's holy one will not be abandoned to the place of the dead. God will raise him up. It is not possible, says Peter, that death could have held the Lord of glory. And the Church – those who are in him – share in that resurrection. That's why the resurrection of Jesus is so important to the Church. If you abandon the resurrection of Jesus you abandon your hope of resurrection. Death once more becomes an enemy. Death once more becomes something to fear, and once more causes you to have no escape.

So there is the past reference – life out of death. His historic, and historical, victory on the cross is *our* victory.

Victory in the present
We live in a world in which we are faced day after day with the realities of death. How do we live in the light and the power of the resurrection? How can we show that we are a community against whom death has no power? How can we show that the gates of Hades are not prevailing against us?

'After all,' someone might say to you, 'you'll die like the rest of us.' How do we witness to life then, in the midst of death? Certainly not by doing what the majority of people do, which is to try to forget all about it. Someone has said that the fear of death is so natural that all life is one long effort not to think about it. Isn't that true? But death is the one truly democratic institution; one man, one death.

I believe that as Christians we need to help people face up to and have victory over the fear of death. But that peace only comes when they've grasped the significance of Jesus and his resurrection.

Someone in the congregation rang me up one day and said that the one-month old baby of a friend had just died. The mother had asked the question 'How can I know that my baby is with God?'

What, as Christians, can we point to in such a situation? Surely to the resurrection of our Lord, as positive proof that resurrection is a reality; that there is hope beyond death. But when we bear witness in that way, let's be very careful not to imply that somehow such a belief removes the reality of mourning, or that the death of a loved one ceases to be painful.

There is always an air of unreality about Christians who are so anxious that their belief in the resurrection should be noticed, or so anxious that a Christian funeral should be triumphant they fail to be truly human in their feeling of loss and loneliness. The witness to the power of the resurrection is completely lost if people find it impossible to identify with the bereaved.

Of course a Christian funeral should be a wonderful occasion, a wonderful statement of faith that the deceased is with the Lord and will enjoy him for ever. But it is also necessary to show that the Lord recognises that we are human, and that for those who remain there is great pain and great suffering; and to show that even so, he is also the Lord who is able to comfort and draw close to them in their sorrow.

This is life in the midst of death; life which brings strength to cope with the death of others here and now; life which brings strength to us as we face our own death.

Some years ago there was a disaster at a mission station in Thailand. A large number of Christian missionaries and their children lost their lives in a road accident. Not very long before it happened, we at All Souls had sent a doctor and his family back to the hospital at that mission station. When the accident happened the doctor lost his wife and two children. He has just one son left now.

Another member of our church who was also a doctor was due to go to Thailand to visit the hospital shortly afterwards. As he arrived at the airport in Thailand, the doctor who had just lost his wife and his two children greeted him, saying 'Rex, this must be terrible for you.'

Imagine when you've lost your wife and two children, saying – or even thinking – how terrible it must be for someone else coming into a situation, and being able to think about other people at such a time. That sort of concern can be only shown by somebody who has learned something about life in the midst of death; who is experiencing resurrection life; who in a tragedy can and does still look to God.

One final observation in this section. Why is it then, if we have this victory over death, that Christians still have to suffer physical death? Why, if Jesus is supposed to have reversed the situation, don't we just go straight to heaven?

It seems to me that the answer lies in the fact that though we have indeed been saved from spiritual death, from the exclusion from God's presence which our sin would have brought us, nevertheless we remain human. And because we remain human, we still have to go through physical death.

But there's a wonderful difference. Now, instead of death being the gateway to judgement and to condemnation, it's become the gateway to life in the closer presence of God. The sting of death, as Paul says in 1 Corinthians 15:54–57, has been withdrawn. We can go through the gates of death not finding that they clang behind us never to reopen, but rather finding that they open out again into eternal life – life in the midst of death. And in this matter just as in so many other things, we Christians must be signposts to others, pointing them to another reality, a reality beyond the physical world.

Victory in the future

The Church will finally enjoy life without death. It will experience the only future that will survive until the end of the world. There's a final victory for the Christian which we look forward to, when death will be no more.

In Revelation chapter 21, when John gets towards the end of the vision that he's been seeing, there's a description of heaven. I'm always struck by the way that the description is in terms of negatives – the things that are going to be no more. There'll be no more pain, no more crying, no more mourning – and no more death.

Death will be no more because, as is depicted in the previous chapter of Revelation, death and Hades will be thrown into the lake of fire. It's a graphic description of the end of one of man's enemies. And thereafter there will no longer be a need for the wages of sin, because all sin will have been purged for ever.

Remember Paul's majestic words, in which he foretells what will happen at the end of time:

Lo! I tell you a mystery. We shall not all sleep, but we shall all be changed, in a moment, in the twinkling of an eye, at the last trumpet. For the trumpet will sound, and the dead will be raised imperishable, and we shall be changed (1 Cor. 15:52).

I don't know about you, but I can never hear those words read without hearing Handel's music as well. There's part of me which will be quite surprised, when the final trumpet does sound, to hear that it's not playing Handel's music!

But there follows in that chapter that tremendous description of the return of our Lord and the beginnings of the life without death. Let me just point you to three things which there are there.

The dead will be raised imperishable. Death can't hold them. Even those who died in Christ and apparently are in the place of the dead will not be held; they will join Christ. The dead will be raised imperishable. They'll come with Christ in his triumph-train.

Those who have not yet died will become immortal. Death will not claim them. They are in Christ, and they will meet him on his glorious return.

Death itself ceases to be a threat. It's swallowed up in victory, says Paul, and it's the victory of Jesus that swallows it up. No wonder that he says 'Thanks be to God, who gives us the victory in our Lord Jesus Christ.' God has fulfilled the law in Jesus. Jesus has broken the power of sin, he has broken the bonds of death. The victory is his, and because we are in him, the victory is ours. From that moment on it's life without death for all time, for all the Church.

The Church, then, is the body of people against

whom the power of death will not prevail. The Church is the body of people who are in Christ and so share his resurrection and his new life. It is the body of people who are living in the midst of death, but showing death to be a spent force. It is the body of people who are looking forward to the final trumpet call which will be for them the beginning of life without death.

4

The cost of membership

Roger Simpson

Then Jesus told his disciples, 'If any man would come after me, let him deny himself and take up his cross and follow me. For whoever would save his life will lose it, and whoever loses his life for my sake will find it. For what will it profit a man, if he gains the whole world and forfeits his life? Or what shall a man give in return for his life? For the Son of man is to come with his angels in the glory of his Father, and then he will repay every man for what he has done. Truly I say to you, there are some standing here who will not taste death before they see the Son of man coming in his kingdom' (Matt. 16:24–28).

I want to begin by quoting a story told by David Watson: a challenge that a Communist once threw out to a Christian. This is what the Communist said:

The gospel is a much more powerful weapon for the renewal of society than is our Marxist philosophy. But all the same, it is we who will finally beat you. We Communists do not play with words. We are realists, and seeing that we are determined to achieve our object, we know how to obtain the means. Of our salaries and our wages we keep only what is strictly necessary and we give up our free time and part of our holidays. You however give only a little time and hardly any money for the spreading of the gospel of Christ. How can anyone believe in the supreme value of this gospel, if you do not practise it, if you do not spread it, and if you sacrifice neither time nor money for it? We believe in our Communist message and we are ready to sacrifice everything, even our life. But you people are afraid to even soil your hands.

Brother Andrew was once speaking of a time when he was sitting with another Christian in a bus in Saigon in Vietnam. As they were travelling on the bus, they saw a man carrying a basket walk out in front of the bus. It was during the time of intensive fighting and constant Viet Cong guerilla attacks.

'Watch out!' said the Christian. 'In that basket there may well be a bomb.'

'Why are you so afraid?' said Brother Andrew.

'That man may be a Viet Cong who will throw himself and the basket under the bus,' came the reply. 'He doesn't mind if he dies – I do.' Brother Andrew commented on this incident, that to him it summed up the ineffectiveness of so much of the Church today. How many Christians are willing to lay down their lives for Jesus Christ?

Now, the text considered here (Matthew 16:24) is entirely relevant when read against that background, because until we begin to take these words of Jesus seriously, we will not see the situation in our own country significantly changing. It is very exciting that many people are turning to Christ in our country. But until we begin to take seriously the words that Jesus says here, we can't expect the gospel really to spread.

In verse 24 we have a clear statement of what is involved in becoming a follower of Jesus, and of joining his people. It's a very challenging, searching statement that Jesus makes. If we put it into practice, our lives would be transformed by it.

This statement 'If any man would come after me, let him deny himself and take up his cross and follow me' is one of those statements that Jesus used on many occasions. It's essential truth, and he repeated it again and again. It comes in all the synoptic Gospels; it occurs twice in Matthew, twice in Luke and once in Mark. And once it was given by Jesus as a warning to those who were thinking of following him, but who hadn't counted the cost. And Jesus specifically warns people of the danger of that in Luke's Gospel, where he says;

> Which of you, desiring to build a tower, does not first sit down and count the cost, whether he has enough to complete it? Otherwise, when he has laid a foundation, and is not able to finish, all who see it begin to mock him, saying, 'This man began to build, and was not able to finish' (Luke 14:28–30).

Now the trouble is that the Christian landscape is filled with half-finished towers, left by people who started to follow Christ and didn't count the cost first. I remember speaking to somebody at Sussex University when I was a travelling secretary for the Inter-Varsity Fellowship. I met her in the bar, where we'd just shown a film-strip, and she said to me 'I tried Christianity, and it didn't work.' When you meet people like that who try but don't really count the cost, it's very difficult to speak to them about Christ.

The other thing I want to say, just by way of introduction, is that Jesus never promised that the Christian life would be easy. And these words in Matthew 16:24 are a clear manifesto of what's involved in becoming a Christian and in following Christ.

Somebody rang me up just two days ago. She said to me 'Roger, I'm thinking of becoming a Christian.' Now I hadn't finished preparing this text, but I almost said to her 'Have you read Matthew 16 verse 24?' Because if you want to follow Christ, then it means that you're going to have to live a life of self-denial. It will involve taking up your cross and following Jesus wherever he leads you. So it's going to be hard. And yet it is also the most exhilarating life that one can live. There's no other life to live but one for Jesus Christ.

So I find myself increasingly in the position where I am encouraging people to think through the cost of following Christ, to consider the cost of membership, before suggesting to them that they follow Christ and join his Church.

But what exactly is the cost of membership? To help us in this, there are three statements, three points we can find in verse 24.

Let him deny himself

Jesus says 'If any man would come after me, let him deny himself.' Quite simply and straightforwardly, this means saying 'No' to yourself and saying 'Yes' to Christ. That's what it means to deny yourself. It means being able to say, as Paul said in Galatians, that 'it is no longer I who live, but Christ who lives in me' (Gal. 2:20). You cannot live both for yourself and for Jesus Christ. The New Testament says so. You either live for yourself, or you live for him.

I often use the following illustration of this when I'm talking to people. I draw a circle, and in the circle I draw a throne; and I say 'You can either occupy that throne yourself – or Jesus Christ can occupy it. You can't both be on the throne.' Jesus says that if we live a life of self-denial, then – as promised in verse 25 – we will find real life. Look at verse 25: 'For whoever would save his life will lose it, and whoever loses his life for my sake will find it.'

In other words, he is saying, 'If you deny yourselves in order to live for me, you will find the real meaning of life.'

I can think of many people I've met who don't believe this. They imagine that by hanging on to their own interests, they will be fulfilled. And they discover in the end that if you do that it simply leads to deep disappointment. But those who deny themselves and live for Christ find life in all its fullness.

To apply this, let us look at the character called Demas.

Paul says of Demas in his second letter to Timothy, that he had fallen in love with this present world and had deserted him (2 Tim. 4:10). Demas, who had begun so well, ended his Christian life as a deserter.

Now why did Demas do that? It occurs to me that probably he had never really counted the cost. He might have been one of the disciples who had got swept into the kingdom on a tide of emotion, and then as things had got difficult, and he encountered the unpopularity, the loneliness, perhaps even the imprisonment, he'd eventually given up and he had deserted Christ.

Or perhaps it was simply that he was approaching middle-age; that as he'd grown older and wearier, he had lost his first love for Christ. Beware of the perils of middle-age! It's so easy to lose your love for him in your middle years. It may have been that Demas loved a life of comfort and ease more than he loved Christ. In other words, he loved the easy way more than the hard way.

Beware, as you get older, of settling down in the Christian life, or, to put it another way, beware of a Christian faith that costs you very little. If it doesn't cost you very much, it's probably not worth very much.

Demas then stands out as a great warning. If you call yourself a Christian, you must be ready to live a life of self-denial, or your love for Christ will wane and pall.

Let him take up his cross

The second thing that Jesus says here is that 'If any man would come after me, let him deny himself and *take up his cross*.' Let's be clear that Jesus was not talking about some affliction that has to be borne. He was instead talking about the sacrifice that is involved in following him.

We don't hear very much about 'sacrifice' today. We often give the impression that the Christian life is a life of never-ending joy and peace. Of course there is a sense in which that is true. But if you miss out the element of sacrifice, you are not being true to the picture that the New Testament gives.

When Jesus talked of taking up your cross, he was using a very vivid picture. In Jesus' day, the Jews were all too familiar with crucifixion. For example, Judas the Galilean had led a revolt against the Romans. His men had raided the armoury. The Romans punished them by burning their town to the ground. Then they sold the wives into slavery, and the men who had been involved in that insurrection – two thousand of them – were crucified. They actually lined the streets with those crucified Jews. When you walked down the street and saw people literally taking up their crosses in Jesus' day it was a very powerful picture. You knew that that person was about to die a very painful death.

So when Jesus says that if you want to follow him you have to take up your cross, he is saying very vividly, 'If you want to follow me, you've got to die to yourself and it has to be as definite as crucifixion.' Crucifixion is painful, and so is dying to yourself; to a life of ease and pleasure, in your service of Christ and in your service of your fellow-men.

It's interesting that Luke, when he records this statement, adds with a flash of insight a single word. He says, let him take up his cross 'daily' (Luke 9:23). This emphasises the fact that it's a day-by-day sacrifice that Jesus looks for from us, not just the great moments, when we come forward at a meeting or stand up in a tent, or something like that but the day-by-day sacrifice of ourselves, saying 'No' to ourselves and 'Yes' to Christ. That's what it means to take up your cross daily; it means saying each day, 'Lord Jesus, I want you to be on the throne today. I want to live for you and not for myself.'

Now let me be quite blunt with you. It's very easy in a large church to come along week by week and to really enjoy the worship. It's lovely to come and praise God and meet people afterwards. And yet you can do that, week by week and do absolutely nothing for Christ. If you're not involved in any sacrificial way, you become pew-fodder.

Let me give you some examples from the church at All Souls. We have probably about a thousand people at our Sunday evening services, and in the morning services, about eight hundred. Do you know how many people we can get out visiting in the parish? About twenty if we're lucky!

I know there are many visitors here. I know many of you come not to hear me but to hear the choir and the music. But that's appalling, I think – that we can only get that many people from a congregation this size who are prepared to get out on a Wednesday night and go visiting.

Do you know, there are lonely people in this parish who never get visited? There are people dying, spiritually speaking, within a stone's throw of this place; and we're packed. And you know how many come here from the parish? Hardly anyone, a trickle.

Do you know how many people we can get to

help at a folk tea once a month on a Sunday afternoon – who'll go out in the streets and invite people in from the street? Do you know, some people get converted by being invited in off the street? Many have nothing better to do on a Sunday afternoon than to walk up and down Oxford Street. And some of them have been fished in here, and they've been converted. Do you know how many Christians are prepared to go and fish for people like that? If we're lucky, fifteen.

Do you know how many people from overseas come here on a Sunday morning? Literally hundreds, and also on a Sunday evening too. Do you know how many people we can get to open their homes once a month to entertain overseas students to give them a meal? Four couples, in a congregation of a thousand. My vision is that tens and tens of homes will be reaching out and opening their doors – and it's hard work. You talk to people about running an open home, it's jolly difficult. You've got to go and visit people, you've got to draw them in.

The club-house needs more helpers. We need help for the old people's visiting. We need people who will sacrifice their time and their energy.

So that's the second thing; we must take up our cross.

Let him follow me

Joining the Church is not just a matter of denying yourself or living a life of sacrifice. It involves following Jesus. That means obeying him.

Did you know that the word 'follow' is used twenty-three times in Matthew's gospel? Jesus told the disciples to follow him. He said 'If you follow me I will make you into fishers of men.' He told the rich young ruler to sell his possessions and 'Come and follow me.' And he said to Matthew, 'Follow me.'

I remember when I was very young playing a game called 'Follow my leader'. You all used to get into a line and whatever the leader did you did; even if it was ridiculous, you did it. We did some pretty ridiculous things!

Joining the Church and becoming a member is always a case of following our leader, though not in any ridiculous sense. Our leader is Jesus. Following him means, doing what he says. It means doing what he wants and going where he wants us to.

Are you prepared to do this? Because that is what being a Christian means.

5

Excellent

The need for discipline

Andrew Cornes

If your brother sins against you, go and tell him his fault, between you and him alone. If he listens to you, you have gained your brother. But if he does not listen, take one or two others along with you, that every word may be confirmed by the evidence of two or three witnesses. If he refuses to listen to them, tell it to the church; and if he refuses even to listen to the church, let him be to you as a Gentile and a tax-collector. Truly, I say to you, whatever you bind on earth shall be bound in heaven, and whatever you loose on earth shall be loosed in heaven (Matt. 18:15–18).

As we come to these verses in Matthew 18, we come to a difficult and complex subject. I'm very conscious that there are many loose ends, and many things I'd like to say more about, as we look at the topic of 'the need for discipline'.

Without discipline, any society disintegrates sooner or later. You see this in schools, factories and political parties. You see it in the recent history of countries like Uganda or Poland. You see it in international alliances. And you see it in the Church.

Where there is no discipline in the Church, moral

and doctrinal anarchy reigns. In 1963, a bishop wrote a book called *Honest to God*. It cast doubt on a great deal of what traditional Christianity stands for. It made the non-Christian world think that Christians didn't know what to believe, and the Church didn't lift a finger to discipline the bishop.

Fifteen years later, a number of theologians — most of them ordained — wrote a book attacking the doctrine that Jesus was God in the flesh. The authors and publishers deliberately generated a great deal of publicity and controversy. Once again, the Church did nothing.

On a more local level, I visited a church in Reading. (I ought to say that the examples that I shall be giving in this chapter are all true, but I have changed some of the minor details.) The clergyman kept in his study photographs of good-looking young boys, clearly designed to be sexually attractive. Several people knew, but nobody took any action at all.

Whether at national level or at parish level, a church which refuses to take its responsibility seriously and to discipline its members when necessary, is bound to be weak. Eventually it will collapse. That is why this passage, where Jesus talks about discipline, is so important, and why we need to study it in detail.

Before we do, we need to face one question. The examples I've given so far are what one might call public offences; sins which, one way or another, affect the whole church. But Jesus in verses 15 onwards seems to be talking about personal offences, where we personally are sinned against. So, can we apply this passage to the kind of public sins I've mentioned so far?

Two points need to be made. First, it is quite true that Jesus here seems to be speaking about personal offences. Actually in verse 15 the words 'against you' are left out in the best manuscripts, but in any case the context makes it clear that that is what Jesus means. In verse 21, Peter responds to Jesus' teaching by asking 'Lord, how often shall my brother sin against me and I forgive him?' And the parallel passage in Luke 17:3–4 makes it clearer still that Jesus is speaking about personal offences.

But later in the New Testament we find that Paul seems to argue that the same procedure, which Jesus recommends here in Matthew's Gospel, should be used in the case of a public offence. In Titus 3:10 he talks about those who are 'factious' – that is, those who stir up controversy and quarrels within a church – and that is certainly a public offence, not a purely personal one. Paul says, 'As for a man who is factious, after admonishing him once or twice, have nothing more to do with him.' That seems to be the same procedure that is being advocated here; a two– or three-stage discipline, ending in exclusion from the fellowship.

Of course there are offences that need to be brought before the church immediately, such as the man mentioned in 1 Corinthians 5, who was living openly in incest, or a case of a church official embezzling church funds. But from the New Testament I conclude that wherever possible, discipline should follow the guidelines here, whether the offence is personal or more public.

And here Jesus lays down three stages in the disciplinary process.

√ Stage 1: A private conversation

'If your brother sins against you, go and tell him his fault, between you and him alone. If he listens to you, you have gained your brother' (verse 15).

So often, if we find out that someone is sinning, we either do nothing about it – 'That's his affair,' we think – or we reluctantly write to the vicar and bring everything out into the open. But those aren't the options at all. We should start, says Jesus, with a private conversation.

Jesus in this verse says three things about that first step. Firstly, *it must be done*. Jesus says quite clearly, 'If your brother sins go and tell him his fault.' Of course that is the last thing we want to do, and we begin to make excuses. We say we're not confident. 'It's none of my business' . . . 'I wouldn't know what to say' . . . 'It needs to come from an older person.' Or we say that we wouldn't achieve anything, that 'it would only destroy our friendship, nothing more. He would never take it coming from me. It would probably just drive him away from the church.'

A Baptist minister rang me and said this about his congregation. 'Standards around here are very low. There's so much lying, stealing, adultery, fornication, but I can't really say anything. It would seem as if I were getting at them.' Faced with Jesus' command, those words are shown up for what they are, mere excuses. It's up to us.

And it doesn't just apply to ministers. Jesus' words here are addressed to all Christians. It's up to us to confront sins where we know it to be present. So if you know that a Christian girl is sleeping with her boyfriend, if you know that a man is lying to the Inland Revenue, if you know that a member of your fellowship group is spreading rumours about the group leader, you cannot shirk your responsibility. 'Go,' says Jesus 'and tell him his fault.' It must be done.

Secondly, *it must be private*. And Jesus really lays this on the line. Verse 15: 'If your brother sins go and tell him his fault between you and him alone.' Now this again goes right against our natural inclination. Suppose you discover that a person has been talking against you behind your back. You're hurt – and isn't your natural reaction to talk about it to one of your friends? Suppose you discover that a Christian whom you know is living a double life. Perfectly respectable in church, but in private carrying on a number of casual homosexual relationships. Isn't your first desire to tell someone else about it, to get it off your chest? But no, says Jesus. You should go to the person himself, and your discussion should be between you and him alone.

Suppose you saw someone steal some money. You confront them, they repent. You are entirely convinced that this was a one-off event and there is no reason to think that this will be repeated. Then nobody else should ever know. All desire to tell it to someone else should be resisted. 'Go' says Jesus 'and tell him his fault between you and him alone.' It must be private.

And third, *it must be healing*. The point of confronting the man should only be to heal his relationships; his relationship with God, that's the point of verses 12 and 13, where Jesus talks about the search for the sheep who is gone astray; and his relationship with you. Verse 15: 'If he listens to you, you have gained your brother.'

Imagine now that you discover someone's been spreading very nasty stories about you. In what mood do you go and talk to him? In a fury, deter-mined to 'give him a piece of my mind'? Not if you follow what Jesus says. Or suppose you discover that another man has made inproper advances to your girlfriend or fiancé. Of course you are deeply upset for her. But do you storm at the other person and refuse to talk to him again? Not if you do as Jesus commands. Of course we will need to be firm. Jesus says 'Tell him his fault'. But the purpose is to gain your brother, to heal his relationships, with you, with God and with anyone else involved.

So stage one, says Jesus, is a private conver-sation, and we hope it will need to go no further. But what if it does have to? What if the offending Christian refuses to listen to you?

Stage 2: Small group confirmation

'But if he does not listen, take one or two others along with you, that every word may be confirmed by the evidence of two or three witnesses' (verse 16).

This was a principle of Jewish law. One witness alone was not enough. He might be biased or delib-erately lying or simply mistaken. Two, or better, three witnesses had to give evidence if a charge were to be sustained. And Jesus says that the same principle should be applied in church discipline. He's not demanding eye-witnesses of the sin, but he says that before the whole church is told, the man should be confronted once more in the presence of one or two others. You can see why.

Suppose – to give a purely hypothetical example – that in your church mid-week young people's club a number of girls have been receiving suggestive letters. You think you know who's done it, and you confront the man privately. He stoutly denies it. It would be quite wrong at that stage for you to tell the whole club committee your conviction and bring the accusation right out into the open. You might be wrong, and the man would inevitably be under suspicion thereafter.

So, 'first,' says Jesus, 'you are to take one or two others and in their presence confront the man again.' If he again denies it and if they are unconvinced by the explanations he gives of your evidence, if (to use the word here) what you say is 'confirmed' by the opinion of others, then and only then should the whole of your club be told.

There's another reason why we mustn't miss out this second stage. The whole thrust of this passage is that discipline should be exercised in as private a way as possible. The man may wriggle his way out of it with you alone, but with others present he may be shamed into confession and repentance.

In my last church a friend of mine loaned someone some money. Whenever he asked for it back the person somehow got out of it. Eventually my friend took me and another and in our presence confronted the man who had borrowed the money. My friend had the sum returned to him within twenty-four hours, and it was unnecessary to bring the matter before the whole church.

But what if this second stage of confrontation

fails? Well, in that case, says Jesus, there is a third stage.

Stage 3: Action by the local congregation

'If he refuses to listen to them, tell it to the church; and if he refuses to listen even to the church, let him be to you as a Gentile and a tax collector' (verse 17).

'The church' here is the local congregation – in the early days covered by the New Testament, a small handful of men and women. Churches of a thousand or more were not envisaged. So I think we may say, since the whole thrust of the passage is to tell as few people as possible, that if the offence only affects the fellowship group, only the fellowship group need be told. If the offence is committed within the context of the young people's group, only the young people's group need be told. And so on.

Hence, to go back to our mid-week young people's club: if someone is going round borrowing money off club members, and after being confronted continues to do so, the whole of the club membership should be told. But if there's no evidence that he's asking for money from other church members, there's no need to publicise it in the church as a whole. It is in this sense that I use the phrase 'the local congregation', whether that congregation is a beginners' group, or a training programme, a young people's group or a whole church.

Jesus says three things about this stage of discipline. First, *the congregation must know*. The local group must be brought in at this final stage of Christian discipline. It must not be a decision taken in secret by the leaders.

I was once a worker in a church in which a lady was causing a great deal of trouble in a fellowship group by constantly spreading criticism of the leader. The leader felt, rightly, that discipline needed to be exercised. He confronted her. She made excuses but went on exactly as before. So he took it to the staff and the staff and the fellowship group leader decided that the lady should be expelled from the group. But the group itself never had the situation explained to them. The desire of course was to hush the whole incident up. But the result was that the lady went round the entire fellowship group, and by a series of lies got the majority on to her side. The mistake was a simple one; the group had not been told. And the New Testament is clear throughout, that when it comes to the final stage of discipline the local congregation must be informed and involved.

Of course, the hope is that when the whole group knows the situation, the offending Christian will at last repent. But if that too fails, Jesus' second point in this verse has to be followed. *The congregation must exclude.* Verse 17 says 'And if he refuses to listen even to the church, let him be to you as a Gentile and a tax-collector.'

Let me make one thing clear immediately. The congregation is not to act like a court. It is for the leaders to decide about the discipline. The congregation is to be informed and to act. That is the pattern in the New Testament. In 1 Corinthians 5:3–5 for example, the church is to assemble but it is Paul who 'pronounces judgement'.

When I was in the sixth form at school a friend of mine was found in bed with a new boy. The house-master assembled my friend's contemporaries and asked us what punishment should be meted out. That was iniquitous. It was not for his peers to decide his punishment, it was for the house-master. And the New Testament makes clear that it is for the church leaders to decide what must be done when disciplining is called for. But if their decision is that the offender should be denied fellowship, to be treated as Jesus puts it 'as a Gentile and a tax-collector' (and this is the normal punishment in the New Testament), then it is for the congregation to carry out the sentence and exclude the one who has sinned.

Roland Allen, the famous missionary thinker, writes that in Third World churches, when someone is caught in gross sin some distant bishop deprives him of *spiritual* support, debarring him from communion and perhaps from the church services. Allen points out that this has no effect at all, because the man has probably lost any real desire for spiritual help. By contrast, the New Testament demands the denial of *social* support, that the man should be excluded from the friendship of Christians; and it is that which will really bite deep. That is what Jesus means when he says 'let him be to you as a Gentile and a tax-collector'.

Let me take a specific example. Suppose you discover a member of your fellowship group is sleeping regularly with his girl-friend. You go and confront him with it, but he justifies himself and says he thinks it's perfectly all right. You bring one or two others and in their presence talk about it again. Again he is adamant. 'There is nothing wrong,' he says. You tell the fellowship group leader and the fellowship group, but he refuses to change his decision. Then, says Jesus, he is not just to be debarred from the fellowship group, but from the company of the fellowship group members. And in that case of course, not just the fellowship group but the whole church would need to be told, because the man would need to be debarred, not just from one group but from the entire church, and from the friendship of any church member. That, however hard it seems, is what Jesus is saying.

And he says one thing more. *God acts with and through the congregation.* Jesus says (verse 18) 'Truly, I say to you, whatever you bind on earth shall be bound in heaven, and whatever you loose on earth shall be loosed in heaven.'[1] In other words, if the congregation through its leaders binds a man's sins to him, pronouncing that he is unrepentant and is therefore being punished, God in heaven will bind that man's sins to him. If on the contrary the congregation through its leaders sees signs of repentance in the man, and so removes his punishment and declares his sins loosed, God in heaven will loose that man's sins.

It is in that context that Jesus says the famous words: 'Again I say to you, if two of you agree on earth about anything they ask, it will be done for them by my Father in heaven. For where two or three are gathered in my name, there am I in the midst of them' (verses 19–20).

1 These words were initially spoken to Peter (Matt 16:19) who was thus given the task of principal disciplinarian in the early days of the Church. Clearly, however, Matthew 18 widens this commission to the entire congregation and its leaders.

Now I don't deny that the truth in the latter verse can have a wide application. We can say when a couple of us meet together to pray, that Jesus is there in the midst. But a small prayer meeting was certainly not uppermost in Jesus' mind when he said those words. It's as if he knew that his disciples would think, as you probably are thinking, 'Who are we to cut people off from the support of Christian friendship?' And Jesus replies that when we are gathered together as a congregation to hear the leaders' decision and exercise church discipline, he is there in the midst. And when the church, verse 19, asks God to bind a person's sins because he or she is unrepentant, it will be done by our Father in heaven. These are very solemn words.

Suppose a member of Sun Myung Moon's Unification Church infiltrates our church here at All Souls and starts taking people off to 'Moonie' meetings. First he is confronted by one man, then by two or three; then the group to which he belongs is told. Nothing makes any difference. So he is solemnly excluded from the church and from the friendship of Christians in this place. Let him not shrug his shoulders and think, 'Who cares?' As the church acts in discipline, says Jesus, God acts with and through the congregation in judgement. That man's sins are bound to him in heaven. Or as Paul puts it twice, 'he is delivered to Satan' (1 Cor. 5:5; 1 Tim. 1:20).

So as we close, let us ask ourselves, what is the passage asking of us in our churches? A greater discipline, certainly. We are called not to conduct a witch-hunt in which we're all out to denounce one another, but to have the courage to confront

72

sin when it's there, to call a spade a spade and evil evil. We are called to exercise discipline, even, where necessary, stern discipline.

But let us not wrench this passage from its context. The hope is that the sinner will repent during the course of that first private conversation, or in the small group. And when he does repent the New Testament makes clear we are to embrace him and restore him to our friendship and our love. Paul in fact once warns the church not to prolong discipline after a man has repented.

Discipline should never, never, cause us pleasure. Always it should give us the utmost pain; always we should be keen to forgive and comfort. As soon as we see any signs of genuine repentance, this whole-hearted forgiveness is to be extended, even though a man has sinned against us personally and regardless of how greatly he has sinned; whether it be (verse 22) seven times or seventy times seven.

honeymoon, having at last managed to get to Sorrento and Rome for the first time in our lives, I stumbled on the fact that Arthur had been to Sorrento ten times, because he liked the sea so much there. The seaside for Arthur – as for most people – means usually a seaside resort. And yet I suppose that the word is just as appropriate to a lonely rock in Pembrokeshire or Dyfed, looking out across the sea. Literally, it means 'the side of the sea'; but it's been narrowed down until it means for most of us 'a seaside resort'.

The same thing has happened to the word 'worship'. It tends to be narrowed down in use, until it comes to mean simply 'an activity in the church'. When I pick up books on worship, they nearly all start off by discussing what happens in a service. Now, I believe that misses the fundamental point of what worship is all about.

So it's right, I think, that we should ask ourselves at the outset what the word actually means. If you have a concordance at home, particularly a good concordance like *Young's* which arranges the words according to their Hebrew or Greek meanings, you'll see that there are various minor words translated 'worship' in the Old Testament, reflecting various special uses of the word; but there is one word that is used overwhelmingly often. So that is obviously the word that we are after, and we need to ask ourselves what it means.

The word is *shachah*. It means 'to bow yourself down'. When 'worship' is used in our English translation of the Old Testament, what is being translated is usually that word. And that immediately gives us some idea of what the word means in its usage in the Old Testament.

Now, what about the New Testament? Again, there are several words that are used two or three times, but there is one word that is used more than fifty times. That's the word *proskuneo*.

When we look up *proskuneo* in a dictionary, we have quite a surprise. *Kuneo* means 'to kiss', and *pro* means 'towards'. The word that's most used throughout the New Testament for worship is therefore the word that says 'to kiss towards', or 'to kiss the hands towards'.

Now what does that remind you of immediately? Some people can recall what we saw on our television screens at the Coronation. Prince Philip, and the others that followed, knelt before the Queen and kissed her hand in obeisance to her authority. And that is exactly what the word means. You can even do it as a child; an enterprising schoolboy in a crowd welcoming Lady Diana once asked her, 'May I kiss the hand of my future Queen?' In fact that was *proskuneo*, though he would not necessarily have known it at the time! When Prince Charles was a bachelor, there was a craze among young ladies to kiss him on the cheek. That was a more open gesture; the schoolboy's request was a sign of worship, of obeisance.

So the fundamental meaning of worship is 'to bow yourself down before', or 'to give obeisance to'. Both meanings are there.

Now once you've got hold of this in your heart and mind, then I think it's logical when thinking about this subject to start not in church, but in your home, your kitchen, your office, your hospital ward. Worship is something far more than the activity that takes place here in church.

Worship in Christian living

Our first passage describes one of the three temptations through which Jesus went; and in this case the battle was about 'Whom will you worship?'

> Again, the devil took him to a very high mountain, and showed him all the kingdoms of the world and the glory of them; and he said to him, 'All these I will give you, if you will fall down [cf. *shachah*] and worship me.' And Jesus said to him, 'Begone, Satan! for it is written, 'You shall worship [*proskuneo*] the Lord your God and him only shall you serve' (Matt. 4:8).

It was one of the big three battles for Jesus, as to whom his life was going to be given in obedience, and that battle was fought out in the deserts of Judea. It was a battle that was in one sense a once-and-for-all battle for him. The battle was won, I believe, in the wilderness; although obviously the devil tried again and there were many subsequent minor skirmishes that went on right up to Gethsemane and the cross itself. But I believe there was this once-and-for-all settlement that Jesus Christ was going to worship his father and not the devil, in spite of the devil offering him all the material possessions of the world.

Now you know as well as I do that for most of us, when we come to Jesus Christ – whether that is gradually or suddenly – we come to that point of realising that we belong to Christ; we begin to join in with the assembly of Christians and to worship him and to thank him for what he's done for us, on the first Good Friday and the first Easter.

And you know that there comes for most of us, subsequently, the point of battle, when we are asked the fundamental question: 'But who are you really going to worship?'

It took me many years to wake up to that. I was glad to acknowledge Jesus Christ as my Saviour, even to be known as someone who was a Christian, and to believe it sincerely with all my heart; but it took me until my early twenties to realise that I was simply receiving from God all he wanted to give to me – but was not prepared to lay my life on the line for him. I realised that I was prepared to say to God, 'Thank you very much for saving me, thank you very much for the grace into which I've entered, thank you very much for the gate of glory that lies ahead, and for heaven, and for the removal of the sting of death, but of course, I'm in charge of my life, thank you very much. I'll take all you'll give me, but remember who's in charge.'

My battle, and maybe yours too, was the battle over 'Whose life is it going to be?' The fundamental temptation, as here in Matthew 4, is whether that was going to be a giving of ourselves to all that the world offers, or a giving of ourselves to all that God requires.

There is no halfway house in the temptation. Jesus made that very clear in his teaching in the Sermon on the Mount. Fundamentally you either worship God at this moment, or you worship Satan. Many people would recoil at that and say 'What nonsense! I don't worship Satan.' But if you don't worship God, then the worship of your heart must be going in another direction; and if it's not going towards God, then it is always going towards material or human things.

The first battle of worship is over my life. Am I really prepared not only to receive what Jesus has done for me, but to bow the knee, to give my life to him? 'You shall worship the Lord your God and him only shall you serve.'

Once you see that, you see that for most of us, it works out in very practical terms.

Let's turn now to a well known passage

'I appeal to you therefore, brethren, by the mercies of God, to present your bodies as a living sacrifice, holy and acceptable to God, which is your spiritual worship' (Rom. 12:1).

Paul does not use the word *proskuneo* here, but his use of 'worship' is essentially according to what we have talked about so far.

Paul sees that in worship the issue isn't always rapidly resolved; and he has to make a plea, that having received the mercies of God, the Roman Christians should then voluntarily give their lives back and lay them at the feet of Jesus Christ.

What does that involve? In verse 2 it involves *seeking the will of God* – 'the renewal of your mind', so that your mind is geared to seek what God's will is for your life and not what you might want it to be. It affects your career, the direction of your life, your openness to what God wants.

There are some people for whom God perhaps has put ten burning bushes on the end of the ditch into which they have put themselves, the rut along which they are going, seeking to call them out into some service for him.

There are others who say to God – and have been saying to him for years – 'I'm prepared to go anywhere.' And God says 'But I like you in London' – or Liverpool, or Edinburgh, or wherever they happen to be living already. And they say 'I don't like London', or wherever it may be. God says, 'You stay in London'.

It's less romantic, perhaps, but it calls for a readiness to say to God, 'I'm prepared to do anything, whether it's here or in other parts of the world, but my life is put at your feet Lord'. Don't let any of us think that if that calling is to stay working in a bank or an insurance company, then that is a second-rate way of serving him. If that is where God wants you to be, that's where you *must* be. And 'it is good and perfect and acceptable,' says Paul.

Accepting the will and purpose of God applies in the very circumstances of life. Think of that incident in 2 Samuel 12, where David pleads for the child that he had by Bathsheba. God's judgement is upon the situation, but David fasts and prays and goes right through the night praying and fasting and throwing himself upon God. Eventually the child dies and they're scared to tell him. They say, 'If he's like this while the child is alive, what will he be like when we tell him that the child has died?' But he discerns what they are saying, and he asks them 'Has the child died?' and they say 'Yes'. And then he rises, and he washes his face, and goes into the house of the Lord and worships (*shachah*) in the midst of this tremendous bereavement and sorrow and shattering blow to his life. He doesn't rail against God, but he kneels and effectively says, 'Your will be done'.

You see, worship is a matter of the will of God, and it's also about *the service of God*, (Rom 12:3–8 see also Matthew 4:8). 'Worship . . . and him only shall you serve.' If you worship God as God, you simply cannot be a passenger in the Christian Church. And there are very practical matters of administration here. We need to be very practical. Some people say to me 'Look, I'd like to do something in the church.' And I say 'Would you mind helping in the catering team?' and they say 'No, I'd like to do something.' And I say 'But making coffee is a very important activity!' But it's not enough for them, you see. And the preparedness to wear the servant's towel, to bake and serve and clean and visit and care and do some of the 'backstage' jobs is sometimes the thing that Christians don't want to have.

In Romans 12:9–13, we find a concern with *the standards of God*. This is also worship. When you have a struggle in your office over whether you can do something you're being asked to do – for example, you're a secretary and you're told by your boss to say he is out when he is actually sitting there at his desk – what do you do? The very fact that you want to battle it out before God, and do what is right and true by God, is worship. It is a submission of the standards of your life to God. When you are called to do something which is dishonest in business practice, or be threatened with the sack, the issue is right there side by side with the temptation of Jesus. Who do you worship? And if your decision is against God's standards, then it isn't an act of worship but a denial of him.

In verse 13 Paul talks about *the use of money*. I hope it is true of many of you, as you fill up that wretched buff form that comes from the Inland Revenue every year, that as you get to the end of it you set down the proportion of what you gave last year relative to what you earned. For most of us, that means a radical overhaul of our giving every April. And what we do at that moment is an act of worship.

So it goes on, in many more areas of our living and our attitude to the world. Worship in the Scriptures is an attitude of living for God.

Worship is a matter of our coming together

If we understand the words *shachah* and *proskuneo*, then what happens in our church at 11a.m. or 6.30 p.m. on a Sunday or at any of our worship services is fundamentally a submission of ourselves to God – a bowing of the knee to him, a kissing of the hand to him.

Let's go back to the Old Testament, to Psalm 95. There are two sections in this Psalm. The first, in verses 1–5, is concerned with *praise and thanksgiving*. It is true to say that praise is *part* of worship, but it's not the same as worship. I find that in recent years I increasingly meet people who talk as if praise is worship, full stop. I hope that you've seen already, by what we've looked at tonight, that that simply cannot be true. And it's interesting that in this Psalm the psalmist spends five verses talking about praise and thanksgiving before he calls people to worship. In Psalm 95 it seems that praise and thanksgiving is an introduction to worship. It is a glorifying of God. Before you come into worship, which is the real submission to God, you stand back to praise and adore him and thank him. These are not mutually exclusive, and obviously praise is part of the total worship.

Now, I believe it is very good to start with praise and thanksgiving, to look at God. It is good particularly if this praise and thanksgiving is focused on him, because that's what total worship is all about. I think there are borderlines in this matter. Some of the choruses and hymns being sung today are not necessarily too much concerned with God.

I was speaking to someone the other day and they said 'Oh you should have been at such-and-such a Christian event, the kids were stamping their feet, waving their scarves, it was just like a football crowd!' But was it worship? It might have been, I wasn't there. It might have been people really caught up with God and this may have been their way of expressing it; but I fear from my own experience, particularly in my younger days, that it wasn't.

But praise really is praise if it is concerned with God, and of course Psalm 95 is. It's concerned with God in creation. He's 'The rock of our salvation'. 'In his hands are the depths of the earth. . . .' Praise is intended to be contentful. That is why the little chorus that the children were taught – 'I am H-A-P-P-Y, I am H-A-P-P-Y; I know I am, I'm sure I am, I am H-A-P-P-Y' is the utter dregs. You don't have to be a Christian to sing it. You can have just had an ice cream soda, or a ride on a bumper car. It is totally devoid of anything to do with Christ. 'All right,' you might say, 'but come on! You are being a bit hard on it.' Yes I am, but simply as an example.

Praise ought to be concerned with God; and as for worship, read verses 6–11. You see what they do? They expand the word *shachar*. 'O come, let us worship and bow down, let us kneel before the

84

Lord, our Maker!' So that as the people came together, there was a physical expression of submission to God. Now I want to say to you, as I want to say to myself; that is what worship is in essence. And if you and I when we gather to worship on a Sunday morning and Sunday evening are not submitting ourselves to God, then you can be the best singer, you can enjoy the service, you can go out and say 'Great, isn't it!' and it isn't worship of the Lord.

We get people occasionally at All Souls who come simply to hear a preacher. One person wrote to me 'If only you'd get those preliminaries out of the way quicker.' *Preliminaries?* That's exactly the word he used, and it's the attitude that the church exists for a particular preacher. 'That's what All Souls exists for,' he said in the letter. He didn't give me his address. . . .

The church does not exist to promote a preacher or preachers or sermons, but the Lord. And what we do from the first moment we come in through those doors ought to be geared towards worshipping God. But it must start before we come through those doors. If we come nattering down the street about everything under the sun and burst into the doors without ever thinking about God until we get in here, it will take us twenty minutes even to begin to move into worship.

So I believe worship begins before you leave your home, or your flat or your digs. It begins, if possible, on your knees as you ask God that as you go and join your brothers and sisters in Christ, you may truly worship him and that the service may be one in which we all can worship him. And so you come down the road ready to worship him; you come into those doors *expecting* to worship God. You don't just simply sit there and say 'Who's on tonight?', but you want to meet with God.

We often have a tension before the service, because there's such a hubbub of friendship that it's very difficult to be quiet beforehand. But the quiet of your heart, the readiness to meet with God, should gear you in to the opening hymn, so that when we come in penitence to worship God you really mean business about repentance and God's forgiveness; and that when you come to the prayers they really are the prayers that you seek to concentrate upon and to echo as far as you can in your own heart and life. So that when we stand to praise, you want to praise God.

Worship (verses 8–11) is also concerned with *the word of God*. Worship is both the submission in all that takes part in this service, and submission in the word itself. And this is why the psalm here follows the theme of worship with the theme of readiness to have our hearts open to the word.

That is why as the word is read, we have Bibles in every seat. And that is why it is important, as the word is preached or expounded that we should be prepared to say not, 'Wasn't that a lousy sermon . . . a good sermon . . . a bad preacher . . . a good preacher', but to say, 'What does God want to say to me through this passage or through this word tonight?' Then we are worshipping. The worship is still going on just as much as when we were singing the hymns and tapping our feet.

It's a terrific subject, much bigger than I can deal with here. But the nature of worship puts a great responsibility on all of us who are involved in the preparation of services. It affects our thinking and planning and praying – regarding the preaching, the music, everything that goes on in the church service. It raises questions about freedom in worship, the use of liturgy, styles and sharing, extempore worship and so on.

But these are all secondary to the fact that we come here to meet with a living God. One of the things about 1 Corinthians 14 that I love is the way in which the outsider comes in and feels that these people mean business with God. And he falls down on his face to worship God, as the Bible tells us, and to declare that God is really among them.

That's what I long for, and I thank God that it is frequently true, in his mercy, that people are touched here by the worship.

So please, every Christian, it's important that you worship. It is an intangible something that springs from the Body of Christ, into something that many non-Christians who come to our services find real. It is often the thing that most attracts them to explore the reality of the faith that we proclaim.

Let me say something about prayer. Let me simply observe that if we accept what I have said – that worship is bowing the knee, kissing the hand, submitting in obeisance to God, that it is a matter of your life, of meaning business with God and wanting to respond to him when we come together to worship in the church – then it must follow that the church that means business in worship means business in prayer. Why is this? It is because in the prayer of our individual and corporate life, we submit again to God, saying 'Lord, without you I can do nothing.' One of the other things that saddens me occasionally is when I hear the leader of one of our fellowship groups say to me, 'A number of our group come to the church prayer meeting, but some just consistently and persistently say "We are not going to come to the prayer gathering of the church" – even when they could come if they wanted to.' This doesn't apply to those who are nurses and students and pray in your Christian Unions and other groups – this applies to people who could come, but who just don't like it. But it's not a matter of liking or not liking, it's the plain fact that without our coming to God as a church and meaning business with him in prayer, we might as well pack the whole shop up.

Why is it that God is meeting with people at All Souls? Why is it that we've got six beginners' groups running parallel, and three 'agnostics anonymous' groups at All Souls? Why is it that a stream of people are being converted at All Souls?

I tell you it's because a lot of people in the church mean business in prayer. And if we cease to mean business with prayer, then the flow will stop. And so I want to ask you: if you don't think it's necessary as a church member to be present at prayer meetings, how do you think the church is going to go forward? It won't be by relying upon the staff, but upon God.

And I want to plead with you to think about it again. In your own life, to go out into the world in your daily work without having literally or metaphorically bowed the knee to God is spiritual suicide. You are entering into the day without the Lord.

Prayer means bowing the knee to him. I would like to encourage people to do that literally. I find in my own personal prayer that actually kneeling is a great help – though perhaps not to everybody. I'd love us to rediscover kneeling in the church again.

So I want to plead with you. In all our living and our coming together and our praying alone and together, we need to be more centred upon the Lord. As the writer to the Hebrews puts it: 'Let us offer to God acceptable worship with reverence and awe; for our God is a consuming fire' (Heb. 12:28–29).

Perhaps it's no coincidence that it was on the Sunday after Easter that one young man by the name of Thomas, having doubted his brethren, bowed himself before the risen Saviour and said 'My Lord and my God!' Perhaps many of us, afresh or for the first time, need to bow our lives before him right now. And that is worship.

Other Marshall Pickering Paperbacks

THE KINGDOM FACTOR

Roger Mitchell

We are living in extraordinary days. The rains of revival are on the way. The cloud is already bigger than a man's hand. All over the world is a resurgence of living Christianity. The coming in of the Kingdom of God in our generation is a real possibility. Whether or not this movement of God's spirit will finally bring the return of Jesus and the universal Kingdom of God will depend on the size of our vision of Jesus, the depth of our fellowship together in the Holy Spirit and the success of our evangelism. This can be the generation.

This is the thrust of evangelist Roger Mitchell's powerful book challenging Christians to bring in the Kingdom of God and to proclaim to a world desperately seeking answers that it is not some vague future hope, but a solid present.

WHEN YOU PRAY

Reginald East

Spiritual renewal has awakened in many Christians a deeper longing to know God more intimately. Prayer is the place where we personally meet God, yet it is often treated simply as the means for making requests for our needs, and offering our stilted, dutiful thanks. In this practical guide to prayer, Reginald East shows how we can establish a prayer relationship with God which is both spiritually and emotionally satisfying. Through understanding God and ourselves better, prayer can truly become an encounter with God, where we relax into Him, enjoy Him, listen as well as talk to Him and adventure into discovering His heart of love.

MY FAITH

Compiler: Mary Elizabeth Callen

Well-known Christians invite us in through their private doors to reveal fascinating glimpses of their most personal thoughts and deepest convictions about their faith.

The late Laura Ashley and her husband frequently turned to the Bible for advice on her growing business. Botanist David Bellamy knows who to thank for all he enjoys in life. At 102, Catherine Bramwell-Booth still lives to spread the message of Christ. Lord (Len) Murray found God in the poverty of London's East End. The presence of Christ transformed the agony of torture into 'a privilege' for Dr Sheila Cassidy. For Anne Watson, God became more real and more mysterious during her husband David's illness and death.

Their moments of peace, doubt, anger and pure joy are common to us all, yet their experiences confirm the uniqueness of God's love for each individual.

FORGIVE AND RESTORE

Don Baker

When a member of God's family, in this case a loved pastor, goes seriously off the rails in his personal life, the question looms large, 'What should the Church do about it?' 'Is it a matter for the church leadership only?' Should the wayward member be asked to leave or just relieved of responsibility? What should the congregation be told?

This book is a remarkable account of how one church dealt with such a highly charged and emotional crisis. It records in honest detail the ebb and flow of hope and despair, uncertainty and humanity, and relying throughout on biblical principles, it picks its way through a tangled mess to find a place of healing and restoration again.

6

The Church's worship

Michael Baughen

Our series so far has been based on references to the Church in Matthew. But as we come to the theme of worship, I want to approach it in a much wider sense than, for example, that passage in Matthew 18:20 which speaks of 'where two or three are gathered in my name'. My reason is in part because the real context of that passage is the discussion of discipline, and also because the whole theme of worship is much bigger than that.

So we're going to look at the theme in a broad way, and I'm well aware that we will still barely touch upon what the Bible has to say about worship. It's a subject I have written about in *The Prayer Principle*, and in that book I also wrote about the subject of praise rather more fully than we can do in the present study.

Worship – its real meaning

Words often take on a narrower meaning than they were originally intended to have. For example, what does the word 'seaside' mean? To our beloved verger, Arthur, it means the place where he goes to have a dip in the briny in his bathing trunks. When I and my wife came back from our second

75

If you wish to receive *regular information* about *new books,* please send your name and address to:

London Bible Warehouse
PO Box 123
Basingstoke
Hants RG23 7NL

Name _____

Address _____

_____

_____

_____

I am especially interested in:
- ☐ Biographies
- ☐ Fiction
- ☐ Christian living
- ☐ Issue related books
- ☐ Academic books
- ☐ Bible study aids
- ☐ Children's books
- ☐ Music
- ☐ Other subjects